HIGH DESERT

André Naffis-Sahely is a poet, editor and translator whose many publications include two collections, *The Promised Land: Poems from Itinerant Life* (Penguin Books, 2017) and *High Desert* (Bloodaxe Books, 2022), and a pamphlet, *The Other Side of Nowhere* (Rough Trade Books, 2019). He also edited *The Heart of a Stranger: An Anthology of Exile Literature* (Pushkin Press, 2020).

His poems have been widely anthologised and translated into Arabic, Greek, Romanian, Italian and Spanish. He has translated over twenty titles of fiction, poetry and nonfiction, including works by Honoré de Balzac, Émile Zola, Alessandro Spina, Abdellatif Laâbi, Édouard Glissant, Frankétienne, Ribka Sibhatu and Tahar Ben Jelloun.

He grew up in Abu Dhabi, but was born in Venice to an Iranian father and an Italian mother. He has taught at Whittier College, Occidental College, and University of California, Los Angeles, where he was the Author in Residence. He is editor of *Poetry London*, a Visiting Teaching Fellow at the Manchester Writing School in the UK, and a Lecturer at University of California, Davis in the US.

ANDRÉ NAFFIS-SAHELY

High Desert

BLOODAXE BOOKS

Copyright © André Naffis-Sahely 2022

ISBN: 978 1 78037 620 2

First published 2022 by
Bloodaxe Books Ltd,
Eastburn,
South Park,
Hexham,
Northumberland NE46 1BS.

www.bloodaxebooks.com
For further information about Bloodaxe titles
please visit our website and join our mailing list
or write to the above address for a catalogue

Supported using public funding by
**ARTS COUNCIL
ENGLAND**

Cover design: Neil Astley & Pamela Robertson-Pearce.

Printed in Great Britain by Bell & Bain Limited, Glasgow, Scotland, on
acid-free paper sourced from mills with FSC chain of custody certification.

for Zinzi

ACKNOWLEDGEMENTS

I am grateful to the editors of the publications where some of these poems first appeared: *Academy of American Poets, Bennington Review, Fifth Estate, Gutter, The London Magazine, The New European, New Statesman, Ploughshares, Poetry, Poetry Birmingham, Poetry Ireland Review, Pratik, The Spectator, The Times Literary Supplement*, and *Wildness*; as well as the following anthologies: *Poets Respond to Covid-19* (Shearsman Press, 2021), *And We Came Outside Again and Saw the Stars* (Restless Books, 2020) and *Field Notes on Survival* (Bad Betty Press, 2020). 'Roadrunners' was recorded for the Poetry Foundation's *Poetry Now* podcast series.

My thanks are also due to the publishers of two pamphlets where some of the poems in this volume first appeared: *Forgotten Californians* (Hedgehog Poetry Press, 2018) and *The Other Side of Nowhere* (Rough Trade Books, 2019). Special thanks to Fred D'Aguiar, Lawrence Joseph, Neil Astley, Alba Ziegler-Bailey, Nina Hervé, Will Burns, Mark Davidson, and Declan Ryan.

CONTENTS

IV: A PEOPLE'S HISTORY OF THE WEST

V: CODA

I

Peregrinations

Hell, man! You've been an exile for years.
And of your own accord, too!

THOMAS WOLFE

testa de fogo ch 'l giasso inpissa

ANDREA ZANZOTTO

The Last Communist

There are, it is true, still a few Marxists around.

Washington Post, November 6, 2017

'We drank no milk for months, maybe a year,'
my mother told me, 'they poured
a famine's worth down the drains;
all talk that summer
was of nuclear clouds
and acid rain.'

Then came the crumbling of the Wall,
and my father's tears –
my childish vision of him
as the last communist,
bathed in the blue
glare of defeat,

the revolution having been televised
and discarded
as yesterday's news.
Three decades and two
recessions later,
the old man

is gone and I sit and sift through
the souvenirs of the cause's
demise: Deutscher's
Prophet, expired
union cards, some
sepia photos

and his final Iranian passport, the Islamic
Republic's seal printed atop
the Shah's lion, history's manner

of illustrating how horrors
beget only
more horrors;

I weep at the sight of his prison diaries
memoirs of my journey to hell,
his miniature scrawling
consuming whiteness
with a convict's
passion for parsimony.

I am tired of murder; each day brings a new Peterloo
and all over the Earth, the fog
of infallibility touches
the ground and threatens
to stay. IT IS BETTER
TO LIVE ONE DAY AS A LION

THAN ONE HUNDRED YEARS AS A SHEEP. Perhaps;
but I'll always choose to side with the flock,
for I know that one day
the veldt will be empty
and even the lion
will go hungry and die.

The Other Side of Nowhere

Thirty feet above the ground, in a warehouse
in the industrial outskirts
of a city we'd never lived in,
I knelt inside the near-empty container

to contemplate our nomadic misery:
mismatched chairs, kitchen appliances
older than me, baby clothes,
framed diplomas, books in a language

my father never taught me *(it would*
have stunted my assimilation)
and in my head, an email from my mother
that read, 'we're doomed, save what you can'.

So there I was, on the other
side of nowhere in sunny Italy... Despite
the technological changes around us,
disasters still travel in telegrams: *Bankrupt.* STOP.

Sorry. STOP. *Homeless.* STOP...
Remember, brother,
when our parents calling us
'global citizens' inspired great hope?

But the world proved too tribal for us
and so your suitcase shall be your only friend
while Shi Huang's fantasy of a Godly Wall
proliferates across the planet.

Weeks ago, two cops in Catania
stung a sixteen-year-old boy from Darfur
with cattle-prods to impart the following lesson,
'whatever the government says,

you're not welcome here.'
As if one needed the reminder...
All across the boot, the green-
shirted faithful lift their pitchforks

to chase the monster of Otherness,
so don't ask me why I love
to leave and hate returning.
(*Is the answer somewhere inside this container?*

It isn't... but remember Cicero's saying,
there's no cure for exile except to love
every city as you would your own,
but the past is always easier...)

When I was young, I fancied
myself Indiana Jones; later,
with erudition, came realer idols:
Petrie, Schliemann, Carter, Kenyon –

but you cannot rescue history from dust –
all you save one day will crumble
in your hand. 'Trash or burn the rest'
I told the warehouse worker

as we rode the forklift back to earth.
Damn whoever said
that hell was down below;
they clearly never went there.

Florence, Italy

14

Folie à trois

After the three of you disappeared,
I slowly adapted to life without you,
but before that came the final act
of our family's international production

of *Failure to Integrate...* Following
your final bankruptcy, I met you in LA
and ferried you south to San Antonio Del Mar,
your last known location. Years later,

I still don't know where or whether to grieve,
but in a way, I won't have to. You always did say
that true migrants ought to be buried upright
like the Kurdish warriors of old, ever ready for battle...

Baja California, Mexico

Nova Atlantis

In the thirty years I've been alive the city's bled half its people and each new decade swallows another step of Istrian stone... From the Zattere to Saint Helena, the winged golden lions still clutch their swords and tablets of the Law, but never all that convincingly; and on Calle del Morion, the only big cat fit to flutter in the wind is wearing a balaclava. *Can you hear him roar?* It is obvious now to all – the wealthy have whored out our house and amidst the Burger Kings and Hard Rock Cafés, I hear an old refrain: *quando el paron no ga cervelo, la casa va in sfacelo*, or, *when the master's got no brains, his household goes down the drains.* While the Lombard kings called us seabirds, we've grown thick fur and turned into water-rats, nibbling on our heritage one miserable mouthful at a time... How fine a grave this green lagoon will make for its childless Queen... What say you now, Marcantonio Bragadin, flayed alive in Famagusta for your loyalty to the Serenissima? What good are screams if there's no one left to hear them?

Venice, Italy

16

Spaghetti Westerns

Noisy marshes outside,
but a desert indoors.
He kept his jailhouse quiet:
a doberman at the gate,

the women seen, but never heard,
their feelings like stogies,
to be chewed on and spat away.
On Sundays, the villains' monologues

were his sermons and gunshots
his church bells. *Beyond the Law,*
The Hills Run Red, Death Rides a Horse,
God Forgives... I Don't! The landscapes

on the screen as empty as his heart,
and the near-absence of dialogue,
intensely satisfying. If only life
might have been edited down

to a ten-minute shoot-out. Occasionally,
bored with thieves and their corny jokes,
he'd oil his guns, mopping his brow
with the bottom end of his wife-beater.

Blood... Death... Retribution...
The Spaghetti Western's Holy Trinity
might have been his prayer, Love
was merely a bonus, a rancher's daughter

to be abducted and brutalised
for the mimicry of affection. Upright
until the end, his body possessed
a henchman's durability: no wound

cut him too deep, and no illness
could lay him low. Years later,
my Aunt Mariella, convinced she could still
hear his footsteps, would pace around

the empty house in the dark, negotiating corners
like some deputy expecting an ambush;
the house was later sold at auction
and the crows did dig his grave...

Montricher

Not the smallest village you've ever seen, but close enough. A handful of white chalets at the foot of the Jura, wide fields of grain, the same six or seven surnames in the nearby cemetery and a Municipal Hall, painted pink, right across the street from its mortal enemy, the Church. The castle that once lent the village its name, long since demolished, is now a thicket of firs, a fitting tribute, perhaps, to Pierre the Kind, an early Lord, who gave his peasants free run of the forest and almost miraculously, expected nothing in return. Centuries later, losing faith in the old continent, Montricher's penultimate Seigneur, the Baron de Poellnitz, a Prussian, penned a letter to Benjamin Franklin: 'I want to be numbered among the Free Men of America' and set sail, not long before Louis XVI met the blade, only to die, bitter and penniless, on his slave-run plantation, somewhere in Ragtown, South Carolina.

Switzerland

Young Romantics

Everyone I knew was homeless, runaways for the most part. One was a grandson of Evelyn Waugh; his father lived off royalties, his son in expectation of them. We slept in the bookshop and the sign above the archway read: 'Be not inhospitable to strangers lest they be angels in disguise.' After its doors shut at eleven, we stayed up, drinking, reading, arguing... once I puked on an autographed portrait of Ginsberg... We lied, stole, ate bruised fruit. Occasionally, one of us would go missing, only to return, days later, like a tomcat. Only Alexander was quiet, he was nineteen and already a veteran of sackcloths and sawdust: Norman monasteries and Québécois logging mills. He was the first to leave, off to a ranch in California, where the nearest town was an hour's drive away: a life of early rises, alfalfa, cattle and poetry. Next I heard, he was homeless in New York, but alive.

Paris, France

Chittagong

This is where the West's ships come to die, dozens upon dozens of freighters, cruise ships and tankers lined up on the beach, resting on the slimy sand, awaiting the blowtorches that will gut them. Twenty miles of coastline have been swallowed up by this post-nautical nightmare... A dead dolphin floats down the Karnaphuli and disappears into the Bay of Bengal. A few miles north of the city, the harvesters trudge through the green toxic mud to begin a long day of work. Today, a foreman fished three human fingers out of the muck, each one belonging to a different hand... Further inland, at Faujdarhat Cadet College, the beige barracks and buildings resemble a country club gone to seed. After my talk, I am handed a plaque bearing the school's motto, *Deeds Not Words*. When I ask the commandant, a veteran of Darfur, about his time in Sudan, he pretends not to hear me, then, hours later, his reply: 'how do you translate the meaning of horror?'.

Bangladesh

Ierapetra

Only the young swim in daylight, while the old enter the water
at night, leaving their slippers on the black sand in the black
of night to wade into the black water. The blind boy on the beach

places his hand on his father's shoulder and follows him into the sea
shivering with pleasure. Only the moon, half-formed, is bright.
All the lamps have been dimmed or switched off entirely,

and on the boardwalk the same sight that greeted me in Abu Dhabi,
scores of Pakistani farmers, lonely men enjoying the breeze,
removed from the crowds they feed and fatten. All visitors

outwear their welcome, and here in Sacred Stone, its most
illustrious passer-by, Napoleon, slept incognito and dreamt
of nearby Egypt, his goodbye note, read: 'so long and thanks

for all the raki', or something like that... Greenhouses scar
the hills above like canker sores. The dam that feeds them
is dry and it hasn't rained all year. Imagine spending all day

toiling in there – like being imprisoned inside a blister, so that
someone somewhere can eat tomatoes in December. On the road
to Myrtos, a bust of Kuypers, 'the Dutchman' who turned

the sleepy fishing town into the plastic hot-house of southern Europe.
They who farm the land should own it too, but when does that
ever happen? Not here, not there, not anywhere...back on the boardwalk,

I watch the lonely men leave, one by one. The old, too, have left
and as the moon reaches its apex, the blind boy places his hand
on his father's shoulder again and follows him out of the sea, grinning.

Crete

22

The Train to St Petersburg

(for Fred D'Aguiar)

They locked us in a train carriage, and turned the key twice.
As the sun set over the Baltic, we left Tallinn's
Teutonic castles behind and hurtled into the taiga,
alone. He was older, bespectacled, but still young, his close-

cropped hair was jet-black, his ochre shirt cut from thick canvas.
Hours later, after the train crossed the border with Russia,
we slowed until we came to a stop by a cabin. Its inhabitants:
three burly guards and two mangy cats, mewling atop a toilet.

The guards stepped inside and asked to see our passports.
'There is problem,' the younger guard said, his eyes
narrowing, as he inspected my companion's American
documents, to which my new friend simply replied 'yes!',

prompting a wild-eyed stare from me he doubtless didn't even
register. Pondering his steely nonchalance as one would the sudden
appearance of a portal into another dimension, the guard,
growing angrier, yelled, 'why are you here?' and, puffing his chest,

my companion replied, 'I've come to reclaim my birthright
as the heir of the Romanovs,' a strange claim for anyone
to make, but even stranger, perhaps, for a Black man.
I'd never seen an adult lifted up by his armpits, but the first

guard picked him up off his seat, set him down, then
ushered him out of the carriage and into the cabin,
lit by a single, flickering bulb... I never saw him again,
but hardly a year goes by without my mind sliding back

to that night, and to him, the Black Prince of Russia –
echoes there of Professor Bill Gordon, the 'American Pugilist',
once the doorman of Petrograd's U.S. Embassy, then,
as testified to in the Senate, sometime in 1919, the Soviet Union's

23

first and only African-American commissar. No trace of Bill
outside of hearsay and rumours – a potential figment
of nightmarish racial fear from America's robber barons
and their cronies in Congress, since Bill Gordon, it turns out,

never existed. More likely indeed the twisting of vowels
and consonants that turned Phil Jordan into Bill
Gordon, the former, the valet-cum-chaffeur for
David Francis, America's final envoy to Tsarist Russia.

Quickly learning the language, Jordan scoured the streets
of the city for food for his master and never
came back empty-handed, one of only two Black men
to set foot in the country since maybe Abraham Gannibal,

Pushkin's great-grandfather. Throughout his time in Petrograd,
Jordan refused to walk out in public with the other Black man,
a Trinidadian named Green, because Green's skin,
Jordan said, was too dark. Six months after Red October,

Jordan and Francis returned to America, and never left it again.
His final wish? For a statue of him to be built in Jefferson City,
'a can of beer in one hand and a bottle of Old Crow in the other'.
His chosen epitaph? 'I never lost a fight in Hog Alley.'

Ode to the Errant King

(for Alia Ali)

Stop, my friends, and we shall weep
over the memory of a loved one,
or thousands, or millions, who can
keep track anymore? Remember this,

that the only oath a promised land keeps
is to make you suffer – and,
these days, every blanket
bestowed, every morsel of food,

every mouthful of water is another
buck in the bank. Long gone
is the lamp that lit
the Golden Door; there are only walls

and chain-link fences and Mylar –
why *Mylar?* Envision its sheen,
the deceptive strength
of that metallised film, imagine it

used for warmth in the cold damp of prisons
– what do you see in its mirror-
like surface, if not
the face of a monster? What is

a human observed though the slits
of a cage, can you still
call them human? What is a great
global city, a great country (whatever

that is) without an island
of tears, a terminal of surrender?
What is life if not Imru's poisoned cloak?
Beautiful to behold, deadly to wear...

Enduring wrongs endure, nothing
changes and so tell me why
I still believe in the journey?
Moving is hope and it shushes the mind

and fills the heart with something other
than fear. Mylar, Melinex,
Hostaphan – names that provide
the illusion of comfort

and safety, of guiltlessness. Is a prison
still a prison if the inmates
have X-Boxes? What sadder
use could there be for that foil,

and its interstellar potential. Whatever
became of solar sails, whatever
happened to us? Consider the border,
any border. If a border

is a war zone, then what do the insides
of our consciences look like?
Therein lies a barrenness
to rival any desert, and soon,

that desert will drink what is left
of the sea. Consider, also,
the sky; bloodthirsty Mars
beckons – how far do you think

will we travel before we rediscover
our bond? How many
rocks and stars shall we visit
until we remember we're human?

II

The City of Angels

I did not choose California. It was given to me.

CZESŁAW MIŁOSZ

Who digs Los Angeles IS Los Angeles!

ALLEN GINSBERG

Welcome to America

'Let's start again from the top:
nothing you told me sounds true.
I've looked at your passport
and there are too many stamps.
What kind of man calls himself
cosmopolitan? You're rootless
and dangerous. I've printed out
your poems and essays and
I want an answer right now:
What are you doing here? Love
isn't a reason and neither
is wanderlust. Why would
she want you? Can you make
enough money? I like thrillers
and mysteries and plots with
a point. Look around you,
we're filled to capacity. This
country's too generous... See
that old man in the wheelchair?
He's been here for days & you'll
be here longer. Nobody reads
anymore anyways. I'm late for lunch
as it is – and if it was up to me,
I'd send you straight back.'

The Year of One Thousand Fires

Early in the spring,
hiking along the coast,
we spot the charred remains
of a giant oak tree,

its hollowed trunk roomier
than most apartments. It is illegal
to sleep here, it is illegal
to be homeless here

and so the poor reside
in rusty RVs at the foot
of this billion-dollar view.
The headline in the newspaper insists:

'America will never be socialist,'
as if that had ever been in doubt...
Everywhere the rapacious harvesting of resources,
but scarcity reigns supreme. Everywhere a resurgent

love for one's country, but no faith
in the meaning of government. Everywhere a newfound
love of God, but a concurrent deadening of the soul.
All day, I read about the Gracchi,

Cato, Casca, Cassius and all night,
I dream of Brutus's final letter to Cicero
before falling on his sword at Philippi.
'Did we wage war to destroy despotism,

or to negotiate the terms of our bondage?'
We have recorded the sound
the wind makes on Mars, but we cannot
listen to one another... All year we binge-watch

an endless rerun of the past. Eighty years
after Guernica, another coup in Catalonia and for
the first time in history, the brightest objects in the sky
are all artificial. A year after Woolsey,

wild mustard returns to carpet the hills,
its fire-resistant flowers bursting out of their sooty stasis.
There will be no hibernation for us,
no sleep except our final slumber.

Maybe the People Don't Want to Live and Let Live

(i.m. Arthur Lee)

Sun-drunk, I roll
along the streets of Los Angeles,
while the radio rewrites
the world as I know it. The Sahara,

it seems, is no longer a desert:
it is a graveyard, while the Mediterranean
they add, is no longer a sea,
it too is a graveyard. Strung out,

I stare at hummingbirds high on sugar
and switch over to Love.
I try to picture you, Arthur Lee, a jazz-
talking child of redlined south central.

You were a prince when vinyl was king,
ditched the alleys of misery to rule the clubs
on the Strip in the Sixties. When the hippies
spaced out, you tuned in, glimpsed the core

of the candy-coated dream: church bombings,
race riots, Vietnam – you sang of the rape
of the American continent from the death of the Indian
to the year of the Cadillac. You worked hard,

fucked the band out of bread, and hid in the hills,
where you tripped far removed from the city's sirens
to write your jingles: 'They're locking them up today,
they're throwing away the key, I wonder who it'll be

tomorrow, you or me?' You peaked at 22, recorded
your last words onto acetate, then laid down to die;
but death kept you waiting a little longer, just in case...
You bore the classic curse of the genius:

trippy before Floyd, funky before Funkadelic,
and punk before those posers the Pistols –
'Oop-ip-ip oop-ip-ip, yeah!' Surrounded by darkness,
you obsessed with re-birth: the album names

said it all: *Da Capo, False Start, Vindicator...*
Doubling down, you shaved your head
and sang even harder: 'I'm young and able,
don't want to set the table'. Nothing worked:

you were too white for the blacks
and too black for the whites. The 1980s
saw you staring into the mirror,
playing the odd gig, nursing your mother...

your second act was cut short by the prison
reforms of the 90s: three strikes and you're out!
They gave you six years at Pleasant Valley,
the kind of saccharine name you always hated...

Fame and flowers came late, as they always do,
and the strings lulled you to sleep on a high.
'Alla God's Chilluns Gotta Have Dere Freedom'
The radio buzzes. The West slowly raises its drawbridge.

The Bond

(for Stacy Hardy)

The dry August air reeks of wood and ash
and the smoke plumes
leaving the rocky bowl of the San Gabriels
sink to kiss the lawn.

The dogs bark themselves hoarse, their frightened
black throats as charred
as the wounded hillsides. No refuge for coyotes,
raccoons, or the striped skunk,

as they scatter like sparks from a camper's hearth.
What is power if not
the ability to dislodge the living from
their synchronous groove?

After six months of death and disease, the rabbits
stir from their nests
in the crevices of rusty engines and people finally
begin to mourn.

On Verdugo, a cardboard placard stapled to
a half-stripped tree,
reads: 'Goodbye, Emilio', or, as the newspapers
called him, John Doe #283,

but nobody's heart's large enough to hold all the names
of the fallen. On either
side of the boulevard, a slew
of recession-raptured businesses:

'to let', 'for lease', 'pray for us' – and even the sign
above the gun-store,
ARMED & DANGEROUS says
'we're through'.

Today, my distant friend, I've only room for questions.
What does endurance mean
if it appears to be endless, what is grass if not gunpowder,
what is this chain of encampments

and shanties hugging the freeway if not humanity's take
on the Great Barrier Reef,
each person a polyp on the coral of concrete?
I think of you in Cairo

and your imprisoned comrades, another tinderbox
awaiting the flint-stone
of hurt... It is late at night,
so let every word

draw blood: everything is not going to be all right.
All my life, an unbroken
string of departures, a litany of leaving, but here
and there, faint glimmers

of meaningful connections, including you, my sister
from another mother,
another father, another world. Perhaps we shall soon
meet again, perhaps not,

perhaps the flowers stuffed into the beaked masks
of plague doctors provided
more comfort than safety, perhaps not,
but what gives us solace

between our first lungful of air and the last handful
of lime? The bond,
only the bond. So, where to now,
wanderer of the wastelands?

El Molino Viejo

A humble, squarish structure, its two
white-washed stories barely
rising out of the earth,
a meagerness redolent

of the old Spanish friars, the dearth of all
decoration indicative
of their distaste for the temporal.
Two centuries ago, in California,

God was both spiritual guide
and entrepreneur: enter
the mission system, where churches
were surrounded by mines, factories, kilns –

holy labour camps in the land
of endless abundance... It could
only be called 'old'
in the American sense, its walls

a summation of the local surroundings,
mud for bricks, pine for beams,
a solid masonry of lime and seashells,
once varnished red with bull's blood.

Impossible now to feel the presence
of the indentured hands that built this place,
except for the gardens left behind
by the sons of Saint Francis,

their green-thumbed *idée fixe*:
that all Indians were idle
and all idleness was evil.
Long since fallen victim to white

people makeovers, I dwelled on the story
of one of the mill's
more colourful residents:
Fannie Kewen, the wife

of the filibustering
Confederate coward,
Colonel Edward Kewen,
who would stalk

the forest at night with a candle
so that the Indians
would think it was haunted –
call it frontier-style

home security
for the racially insecure...
During the real estate bubble
of the 1920s, realtors

sold nearby plots by whispering tales
of El Molino's
buried gold-hoard,
which, of course,

was nothing but bullshit,
just like the boom.
Today, no plaque
preserves its memory,

there are no wildcats in the woods,
while the river
that fed its waterwheel
is lined with trash and shopping carts.

San Marino, California

Rancheros

If the history of Mexican grants in California is ever
written it will be a history of greed, perjury, corruption,
spoliation and high-handed robbery, for which it will
be difficult to find a parallel.

HENRY GEORGE

On feast days, their horses
wore more gold and silver
than entire villages
might see in a lifetime.

Surviving two empires,
raids and annexations,
they succumbed to the
aristocrat's only natural predator,

lawyers, and mortgaged
themselves into extinction.
Theirs was a world steeped
in late-feudal certainty, where God

was in charge, màs o menos,
but the King was only a rumour.
After seventy years of stasis,
their vast estates slipped the cocoon

of the Missions and their Indian
serfs put to 'secular' work...
Descended from soldiers, exiles,
and petty officials, they became

the cattle lords of El Dorado,
whose beef filled the bellies
of 49ers, an economy built on tallow,
where rawhide was money

and boundaries were marked
by a bullock's head on a bluff.
Their final quarter-century
a constant rearguard retreat,

all trace of them finally erased
in favour of small farms,
homesteads and industry.
Their names survive

in a handful of freeways, city parks,
a few adobe houses: Pico,
Machado, Sepúlveda, Verdugo...
Guilty of growing fat

off slavery and genocide,
their greatest sin
in the eyes of modernity?
Slowness of life, slothful inefficiency...

III

High Desert

The desert is not a place... it is a transcendental place, a shadow of a place... in the desert you are excluded from nature, you are in the presence of freedom. What is freedom? It means death and in the desert we are close to that death. The desert is the only place where we can visit death and return home safely.

IBRAHIM AL-KONI

By late 1919, a radical was anyone suspected of being pro-German, a Russian or other foreigner, a person who sent bombs through the mail, a believer in free love, a member of the IWW, a Socialist, a Bolshevist, an anarchist, a member of a labour union, a supporter of the closed shop, or anyone who did not particularly agree with you.

ROBERT K. MURRAY

Roadrunners

In the pink light,
haloes of cloud form over the mountains;
lightning, two valleys away,
then, not an hour later,

the explosion of thunder.
The roadrunners
pecking for breadcrumbs on the porch
have long since fled

into the endless ocean of grass.
Driving in every direction
down licks of red road,
I have lost myself in a militarised topography;

everything named after army units,
generals, scouts, miners...
The Dragoon Mountains,
Cochise Stronghold; defunct

Gleeson and Pearce,
weird, rusty ghost towns, the only
non-derelict structure
for miles, the local school,

its polished windows and well-kept lawn,
a source of great local pride.
No mountain monograms
for these desiccated whistle-stops,

no giant Q or C or W in bright
white paint to mark
the township's still functional
sorta functional breathing, no

carving for them
into the planet's bark;
and thus they are blessèd
to me like no other;

every successful city
is a flimsy affair with civility,
its eternalness, like Paris or Rome,
a slow march to desacralisation.

MAKE AMERICA GREAT AGAIN,
BUY REAL ESTATE! Hail follows rain.
Nearby, the township of Sunsites,
once billed as the safest

spot to survive
the inevitable nuclear winter,
actually topped Soviet Russia's
list of high-priority targets... Enter

the Orange Duck Candidate.
A haboob sweeps across
the Valley of the Senile.
In a week, the mountains

have switched from brown
to purple to green.
The desert is human
endeavour's most fitting graveyard;

the slow bleaching,
the gradual eroding into sand,
the heat stifling sound as it leaps into the air.
IT CAN'T HAPPEN HERE. But it always does.

Sulphur Springs Valley, Arizona

At the Graves of Labour's Fallen

It is intolerable that these itinerants of anarchy should infest
great regions of the West.

New York Times, 14 July 1917

The best plots in the cemetery belonged to cattle-thieves,
cut-throats, bushwhackers, or as any
respectable boom-town would call them,
'our esteemed founding fathers';

but by the north-eastern corner
of that acre of dust
off the Old Douglas Road,
stood the graves of the Wobblies,

tall as cigarette stubs. Time
had made most names illegible,
but what little survived made it clear
that half the world lay buried

here in Bisbee: Mexicans, Greeks,
Slavs and Italians; some fell
down mine shafts, others grew old,
but all died poor; some certainty, at least,

in the otherwise unpredictable lives
led by miners in copper country.
Who ever said that America
skipped its medieval stage?

Nothing was left unscathed by that feudalism...
wandering holy-men, ruthless barons,
armed thugs on horseback,
peasants' revolts, the imaginary, but ever

effective spectre of dark hordes at the gates...
July 12, 1917. Twelve hundred
Americans deported in a single morning:
a posse, a round-up, then a twelve-

hour ride to Hermanas, New Mexico.
'ALL WOMEN AND CHILDREN
KEEP OFF STREETS TODAY'
read the Bisbee Daily Review,

but they were banished too.
Blame public hysteria and spineless
Woodrow Wilson, blame General John J.
(bury them with pigs!) Pershing

and his crusade against Pancho Villa.
Consider, also, the Buffalo Soldiers:
too black to die for their country in France,
but not too black to shoot at Mexicans on the border.

Consider, finally, that no court hears such cases
except that of memory. Come sunset, I speed down
the gulch to Cochise and sing, 'Work and pray,
live on hay, you'll get pie in the sky when you die, that's a lie!'

Bisbee, Arizona

I. W. W. MEMBERS have been murdered.
I. W. W. MEMBERS have been imprisoned.
I. W. W. MEMBERS have been tarred and feathered.
I. W. W. MEMBERS have been deported
I. W. W. MEMBERS have been starved.
I. W. W. MEMBERS have been beaten.
I. W. W. MEMBERS have been denied the right of citizenship.
I. W. W. MEMBERS have been exiled.
I. W. W. MEMBERS have had their homes invaded.
I. W. W. MEMBERS have had their private property and papers seized.
I. W. W. MEMBERS have been denied the privilege of defence.
I. W. W. MEMBERS have been held in exorbitant bail.
I. W. W. MEMBERS have been subjected to involuntary servitude.
I. W. W. MEMBERS have been kidnapped.
I. W. W. MEMBERS have been subjected to cruel and unusual punishment.
I. W. W. MEMBERS have been "framed" and unjustly accused.
I. W. W. MEMBERS have been excessively fined.
I. W. W. MEMBERS have died in jail waiting for trial.
I. W. W. MEMBERS have been driven insane through persecution.
I. W. W. MEMBERS have been denied the use of the mails.
I. W. W. MEMBERS have been denied the right to organise.
I. W. W. MEMBERS have been denied the right of free speech.
I. W. W. MEMBERS have been denied the right of free press.
I. W. W. MEMBERS have been denied the right of free assembly.
I. W. W. MEMBERS have been denied every privilege guaranteed by
	the Bill of Rights.

from a leaflet distributed by the Industrial Workers of the World (IWW)
in Chicago in 1919

Spanish Flu

The final gift of a futile war,
a second chance for death
to make a mockery of prayers
long whispered in the dark.

The first plane-borne virus, the first
headline disease, that century's only
cross-sectional culling, fatal to prince
and pauper alike – its legacy?

Hospitals: the threat of extinction
our only lever for civic reform.
Today, we tremble in the wake
of its innumerable grandchildren,

each one a contender for the Great
Khan's crown, each individual bristle
a village torched by sickness. Remember:
wash your hands while whistling Happy Birthday.

Memorial Day

The crows above fly in murders,
jar-heads hang their stars and stripes,
and all spring, the great war machine
has rumbled on and on. Nine thousand

miles away, herds of nervous cows
are flown across the Persian Gulf
to quench the thirst of theocrats.
A decade following the Great Recession,

the latest statistic: a bottle of bubbly
is popped each second worldwide.
When Napoleon led his soldiers
across the plains of Western Russia,

he made them tow two hundred crates
of vintage wines through blood and snow.
'Today we drink. Tomorrow we pay.'
Not a single drop was ever drunk.

The Great Molasses Disaster

For the first time in the Republic's history, American boots in Europe and after twenty months of war, an explosion in Boston's North End. On an abnormally warm day in January 1919, a ruptured tank unleashed a wave of hot sugar as tall as two elephants over Keany Square. The shopkeepers cried 'It was Anarchists!, the cops instead suspected the Reds, and only a year after Woodrow Wilson wooed the workers in Buffalo, two out of ten workers were on strike. Enter the Sedition Act, the Palmer Raids, loyalty leagues, lynchings, Pinkertons. Justice Louis Brandeis: 'I never knew that Signor Torquemada was so thorough a patriot.' Hello Red Scare, goodbye Emma Goldman. Frank Little, Big Bill, Joe Hill, we won't see their like again... All hail the true lord of Bethlehem, hallowed be thy share price. Didn't anyone ever tell you? The explosion had been an accident after all.

Down to Tucson

...where nobody wants to go in the summer, or so a song on the radio had warned me, yet there I was, south of the Gila, north of Rio Rico, beside a twenty-foot steer-skull, its horns embracing the Santa Rita Mountains. Up there, 'El Jefe', the jaguar, ponders his own extinction, the last large cat to survive the copper mines. Down here, nearly every inch of the state is grazing land, but the plains are empty, only endless miles of feedlots, where the cattle stand shoulder to shoulder, chained to their troughs, immobilised for the final fattening, the air ripe with their reek. As the sky turned from blue to pink, a cowboy scored some speed in the parking lot and on spotting me, offered me a bump in exchange for a cigarette, and sighing in the dusk, not knowing how to feel, my lips could only form a single answer: *why the hell not?*

High Desert

Time to listen to my bones, to seek a stillness
known only to deserts. Pause,
traveller, and behold
this empire of absences: the snowy salt beds

of vanished lakes, the outlines of decommissioned railroads,
the petroglyphs of people
murdered long ago, and, all around
nearly limitless stretches

of cottonwood, willow and mesquite tufting out
of the sand. All day
I drive along mummified freeways
from Amboy to Zzyzx and zip past Cadiz, Bagdad

and Siberia in under an hour's time; the ghost towns
of America's main street,
an unbroken montage
of smokestacks, silhouettes of sidewalks,

the boarded remains of small businesses...
There is no better backdrop
for the mirage
of permanent boom times than the desert,

a landscape, where despite claims to the contrary,
no town was too tough to die.
Once genocide
had cleared the country,

an extractionist lust was unleashed on the West,
the blunt simplicity
of place-names a shrine
to the seekers' obsessions: CARBONDALE,

COPPEROPOLIS, OROVILLE, PETROLIA...
spartan mockeries
of morals and models
left behind and forgotten, towns where Sheriffs

robbed trains at gunpoint, or smuggled liquor
across the border,
only to blame it on the Mexicans...
Next to no sign now of the old tribes,

the trappers, the pioneers, yet no shortage
of jackrabbit meth labs,
tin cans, rusted lawn-chairs,
gas stations and faux-

Fifties diners... dead or alive, each one of them greets me
with the same sign, the same
four planks of wood:
Name, Date of Establishment,

Elevation and Population, the latter always in the single
or double digits.
Exhausted, I lie down
on the sand and warm my feet by the embers

of this final frontier and consider how strange
it is that it's here,
where after decades of rootlessness,
I abandon all cravings for permanence...

IV

A People's History of the West

Pablo Tac (1822–1841)
SCHOLAR & SEMINARIAN

'Thus we lived among the woods until merciful God
freed us of these miseries
through Father Peyri
and seven Spanish soldiers.

In the Mission, the Fernandino Father is like
a king. He has his pages,
majordomos, musicians,
and horses by the thousand.

They made a church, a high tower with five bells
and a cemetery with a crucifix
for all who die here.
No one can dance without permission

of the elders. The garden is full of fruit trees,
but none of the neophytes
can enter the garden.
A great many crows arrive in the evening.'

Mary Ellen Pleasant (1814–1904)

ENTREPRENEUR & ABOLITIONIST

'Some said I was born in slavery,
but as a matter of fact,
I was born in Philadelphia. I never
cared a feather's weight

for public opinion and before
I pass away, I wish to clear
the identity of the party who furnished
John Brown the money to fight

at Harper's Ferry: I'd rather be
a corpse than a coward.
I often wonder what I would have been
with an education. I am not

"Mammy" to everybody in California.
Put. That. Down. I have given
all I had to others;
to my enemies, I say nothing.'

Article Nineteen (1879)
SECOND CONSTITUTION OF CALIFORNIA

'We the People
of the state of California,
an inseparable part
of the American Union,

hereby declare that all men
are free and independent –
all save for aliens,
who are vagrants, paupers,

criminals, invalids,
afflicted with contagious
or infectious diseases.
As such, we shall employ

no Chinese or Mongolians.
Grateful to Almighty God
We the People shall pass
whatever laws may be necessary.'

Denis Kearney (1847–1907)

LABOUR LEADER & RACIST AGITATOR

'I am
an ungrammatical man,
but I thank God for a tongue
and a good pair of lungs.

I stand before you
in this Cradle of Liberty
to stir you out of your lethargy.
Look at your Congress,

all lawyers and bankers.
Our leaders have failed us and now
it is time for good, honest workingmen
to rid us of these gophers and vampires.

Chinamen only dine on rice
and rats. Do you want leprosy here?
If the Constitution were written on a steak
a hungry man would gobble it up.

Beware of land pirates
and moneyed powers. I will not
read any further from the Book of God.
And whatever else happens, the Chinese must go!'

Wong Chin Foo (1847–1898)

WRITER & ACTIVIST

'I was born and raised a heathen,
but my conscience is clear.
Unlike Christians, we do not
organise into dastardly mobs

under the guise of social reform.
In China, strangers
are not everyone's cow,
only good to be milked and then

turned loose. Christians talk long
and loud about how to be charitable,
but it's only talk and
while the poor have all the votes,

they always elect those who yearn
to betray them. If
Denis Kearney
should somehow slip

into heaven, all of God's
angels couldn't keep him
from howling: "Whatever
else happens, the Chinese must go!"'

Ricardo Flores Magón (1874–1922)

EDITOR & REVOLUTIONARY

'I am caught
by the mechanism of a monstrous machine.
My flesh may get ripped open,
my bones crushed,

but the machine
will not stop grinding,
grinding, grinding... I think my case
is a hopeless one. I may rot

like a beast in a cage.
My crime is one of those
which have no atonement: I am
a dreamer and find great pleasure

in sharing those dreams. This is why
I've been branded a felon
and thrown into this hell,
where the darkness

begins to enshroud me
before I am dead. Goodbye,
my good Erma and please offer Ellen my love,
the only thing a captive can give.'

Louise Bryant (1885–1936)
JOURNALIST & ACTIVIST

'I was in the Winter Palace the day it fell. I lived
on bread and cabbage soup. I did not
go to Russia for money and
I was not there for love,

but because I wanted to see the revolution.
How can we fight for
democracy in France and
against it in Siberia? I believe

in socialism and equality for women. A man by
the name of Brown called me
a female Trotsky. Am I
being tried for witchcraft?

I do not want to be treated like a lady, but like
a human being. There will be
violence in America; I suppose
there is a God, I have no way of knowing.'

Buck Colbert Franklin (1879–1960)

ATTORNEY & MEMOIRIST

'Here I am, peaceable and law-abiding and yet
I cannot walk the street; The newsies
are hawking their wares, all about a Negro

assaulting a white girl, the alleged assault
consisted of stepping on the foot
of a white girl on a crowded elevator... I could hear

bullets whizzing and cutting the air. When the eastern
sky reddened, from my office window,
I saw the old Mid-Way hotel on fire, and then

another and another and another building began to
burn. Where, oh where is our splendid
fire department? During that bloody day, I lived

a thousand years at least. "We must fight to make
the world safe for democracy." I repeated
those words aloud and they sounded like hollow-mockery.'

Art Shields (1888–1988)

JOURNALIST & UNION ORGANISER

'This was our town. All the harbour workers were out and vessels
from a dozen lands were strikebound together;
meanwhile, San Pedro was filling up with cops.
Mass raids began and the raids grew bigger day by day.

This was a singing strike: our songs were about the power
of Labour and our power wasn't abstract.
Two thousand seamen sang *Solidarity Forever*;
Upton Sinclair recited the 1st amendment, then Captain Plummer

grabbed the people's novelist and turned him over
to a cop. A lieutenant was barking orders
to men armed with clubs and guns. The case
made global headlines, but it didn't save the walkout.

We circled the waterfront Bastille; our imprisoned
fellow workers sang, "Remember, you're outside for us,
and we're in here for you." Two hundred men or more
were hauled away to sleep on iron floors.'

George S. Patton (1885–1945)
GENERAL & PHEASANT HUNTER

'I urinate in the washbasin and wash in the urinal
because I have forgotten what they look like...
The nearest railroad is twenty-one miles away,
all officers and men will live in floored tents;

I wish to God we would start killing somebody,
somewhere, soon. My dear friend Caroline,
I would be unpatriotic if I aided anyone
in bringing comfort to our country's enemies,

the Japanese in California. I have shot
one or more jackrabbits every day
that I've been here just to keep
my hand in for Rommel. The Mojave

is a wasteland and there is room to burn...
Sitting on a tank watching the show is fatuous –
killing wins wars. Who is as good as I am?
I know of no one... I'm a hell of a guy...'

John Samuelson (18??–195?)
MINER & HOMESTEADER

'Wake up, you tax and bond slaves,
God made man, but Henry Ford
put wheels under him... The key

to life is contact... Hell is here
on earth and nowhere else – we
have made most of it ourselves.

The milk of human kindness ain't got
thick cream on it for all of us.
Ask Hoover... Judge Ben Lindsey

understands humanity. Nature is God.
Study nature... Neither money's
laws nor armies can stop

the human mind. With time, the oceans
grind the hardest granite into
sand... Nothing proven after death.'

Muriel Rukeyser (1913–1980)
POET & PLAYWRIGHT

'Birth date and birth place verified. Did not graduate
and obtained a B-; informants state this school
has communist leanings and subject is listed
as a left-winger poet. In 1933,

Rukeyser drove South with two friends to report on
the Scottsboro Trial and they were held
by the police "for inciting the negroes
to insurrection". The poem "US1"

deals with the disintegration of people in a West
Virginia village riddled with silicosis;
other poems by this author could not
have been written except in a period

of disordered economics. The record further
reflected Rukeyser to be a pacifist;
credit satisfactory, criminal negative.
Will verify subject's present address and activities.'

Richard M. Nixon (1913–1994)

U.S. PRESIDENT & WAR CRIMINAL

'First, we should remove from the payroll
those of doubtful loyalty; easy prey...
I have here a breakdown of twenty-
four hundred people: drunkenness,

subversive activities, sexual perversions
and mental instability; I think you'll
agree that we're dealing with traitors
and rats – and when you shoot rats,

remember this: if you shoot wildly,
the rats may get away. Why is it right?
Because Communism threatens freedom
and we must destroy freedom ourselves.'

V

Coda

Tule Fog
(for Zinzi)

I

After five years of life in the desert, you drive north
as the fog floats over the fields like a ghost,
or a frozen prayer – and rolling
past Delano and Merced, you wonder

what does home mean to you now? Then, the answer
rises out of the cottony gloom: home
is a sleeping bag in a parking lot,
a bedroll in a barn, a blanket laid down

in a ditch, but never a right, never a certainty...
The sun is lost, and everywhere
the feeling that the party is over
fills the air. The king tide of traffic

recedes and a voice on the radio is singing,
'I'm vaccinated and I'm ready
for love.' *'Care team members
are busy assisting other callers,*

*your call is important to us and will be attended
to shortly'*... If happy countries exist,
I've yet to see one, and forty-seven
nations later, my idiot heart still races

at the sweet sound of wheels on the tracks,
but for today, and tomorrow and
three years of yesterdays,
I stay put, wrapped in a fog as dense

as pea soup. What is fog? Fog is water
when it dreams of granite,
when it seeks the illusive
safety of rock, a hologram projected

by the dew. Fog is a phantom bred by fire,
it is the shape grief assumes,
a metaphor for confusion. 霧
is a hill in China where poets

seek refuge from tyrants. Fog is the reaper
that sits on the freeway at night
to harvest its victims, a veil
the sky casts over the Valley

to hide the raw wound that we feed on; fog
is the state of the markets, it is
the love that I feel for my mother,
and the hate that clouds the mind

of her son; fog is a tune that you hear
on the boardwalk as you experience
'some maundering fancy of going out with the tide',
as Jack London put it. There's no escaping it...

II

We flee the city and lose ourselves in its open-air
graveyard, call it 'deserbia', a chain
of dry valleys, a maze of dirt roads,
chicken-wire, yucca trees, and piss-yellow

DON'T TREAD ON ME flags. It was the final act
of the American Homesteader, death-plots
for the Legionnaires of Empire: flatlining hamlets
named after lunatic flyboys, mystics,

cult leaders, paedophiles, prospectors, and other
assorted seekers of extraterrestrials. At dawn,
a lone bugle rips through the rare,
low desert mist, and, like the old man said,

blow, bugle, blow: 'AND NOW, AS THE MORNING CALL
OF THE COVERED WAGONS DIES AWAY
WE BRING YOU ANOTHER STORY OF —'
…loss and displacement. This is where

I was orphaned, marooned, on Baja's foggy beaches,
where my father washed up, broke
and bereft, another mad captain spat out
by the wrath of the sea — and no matter

how many miles I devoured between Tecate and Taos,
that fog never left me. I drove down
country roads, exploring mining camps,
chasing those embers of dead dreams

all the way to the ocean. Nothing breaks your heart
like a small western town: a few
scruffy buildings all clustered together, cowed
by the might of the land,

the devout, frightened believers of a vengeful god:
space — the very space that one day
will reclaim them. They sit here,
patient, self-sufficient, irrelevant,

waiting for that final exodus to put out the lights.
At dusk, in a rented hovel a mile or two
out of town, some relief from the heat
as the sky turns cobalt, then black, then filthy blue.

A thin curl of smoke climbs out of the pit, critters
crawl close to the fire, snakes slither out
of their lairs, and all night long the bugle call
plays on repeat. Perhaps one day I'll stop hearing it.

Central Valley, California

Notes

The found poems featured in part IV's sequence entirely employ words spoken or written by the historical figures portrayed and they have been sourced from their letters, diaries, autobiographies, transcripts of congressional hearings, or, in the case of 'Article Nineteen', from the text of California's Second State Constitution, as agreed on by the Sacramento Convention of 1878–79.

The lines from 'John Samuelson' are taken from writings found by the author on large slabs of rock where Samuelson, a Swedish immigrant, etched his musings during a spell as a gold prospector in what is now Joshua Tree National Park. Samuelson's Rocks may be found in the vicinity of Quail Springs in the Mojave Desert.

The words for 'Muriel Rukeyser' are entirely taken from Muriel Rukeyser's FBI file, released under the Freedom of Information Act.

'Buck Colbert Franklin' is sourced from an unpublished manuscript entitled 'The Tulsa Race Riot and Three of Its Victims' (1931) by B.C. Franklin (1879-1960), a civil rights lawyer of African-American and Choctaw ancestry, as well as the father of the renowned historian John Hope Franklin (1915–2009).

All of these texts are available in the public domain.